I0481216

BITCOIN

A Clear and Simple Guide to Getting Up and Running Fast with Cryptocurrency

ALFORD BENSON

Acknowledgment

I would like to give heartful thanks to my dear friend and colleague Robert Buxton who provided carefully considered feedback and valuable comments. I also owe a very important debt to Arnold Trent whose opinions and information have helped me very much throughout the production of this content.

This book is dedicated to my three years old Mary without whose loving attention this book would have been finished in half the time.

Table of Contents

ALFORD BENSON

INTRODUCTION

Congratulations on downloading this book and thank you for doing so.

The following chapters will discuss bitcoins, bitcoin mining and bitcoin investment. The bitcoin is the dominant form of cryptocurrency or digital currency, a new and innovative form of currency that exists solely on the internet. Unlike traditional currencies controlled by governments, the bitcoin system has no central authority of any kind. It was designed to allow people to exchange money for goods and services without having to rely on governments or banks.

The "crypto" in the word "cryptocurrency" refers to cryptography, the science of making secure codes. Bitcoin transactions are all stored in a public ledger, but there are many different copies of the ledger at any one time. No central authority controls the bitcoin system, so users need some other way to be sure that transactions are safe and can be trusted. When a block of bitcoin transactions is verified and added to the public ledger, it always includes a unique encrypted phrase known as a "hash." Any unauthorized change to any transaction would automatically result in a different hash, alerting everyone using the system that something was wrong. This makes it possible for bitcoin users to trust that all transactions made over the system are always legitimate.

Since bitcoin was first introduced in 2008, the value of a single bitcoin has increased much more rapidly than most people would have imagined possible. As of the writing of this book, a single bitcoin regularly trades for between $11,000 and $17,000 USD.

Following the tremendous growth in popularity that Bitcoin has had over the years, more and more people are seeking to learn all about it. With this book every effort was made to ensure the reader would acquire as much useful information as possible, please enjoy!

CHAPTER 1
INTRODUCING THE BITCOIN

Cryptocurrencies or digital currencies are alternative currencies outside of the control of governments or banks. Until the invention of bitcoin, no one had been able to develop a viable digital currency free of centralized control, because without an authority to oversee the system there was nothing to stop a user of the currency from spending the same digital money twice. Bitcoin's blockchain technology made it impossible to do this, making bitcoin the first decentralized digital currency users could actually rely on. There are hundreds of other digital currencies on the market today, but bitcoin is by far the most popular of them all.

The bitcoin was invented by a programmer (or possibly a group of programmers) using the pseudonym Satoshi Nakamoto and claiming to be a Japanese man born on April 5th, 1975. Despite these personal details, evidence suggests the real "Satoshi Nakamoto" probably lives in either Europe or the United States and may not be Japanese at all. Several different programmers have been named as possible candidates for the role, but the truth is that nobody knows who Satoshi Nakamoto really is.

All we know is that he proposed bitcoin in a paper called "Bitcoin: A Peer-to-Peer Electronic Cash System," which appeared on an email list dedicated to cryptography in October 2008. Nakamoto claimed to have found a way to solve the double spending problem without the need for a central authority by using advanced cryptography, making a decentralized digital currency a viable option for the first time.

In January 2009, Nakamoto released the software needed to carry out bitcoin transactions. He continued to be involved in developing the software until partway through 2010, at which point he stepped away from the project and handed over the source code to programmer Gavin Andresen. Satoshi Nakamoto is thought to own almost $17 billion USD worth of bitcoins, or approximately 1 million bitcoins, but he is no longer personally involved in the project. In fact, no one has heard from him in several years, and no one knows where he is or what he is doing now.

The bitcoin software is open source, and all transactions are recorded in a public ledger held by multiple different nodes or users at the same time. Despite this fact, bitcoin transactions are semi-anonymous. Users are protected by digital pseudonyms or "keys," and there is no obvious way to link a particular transaction to the people who made the transaction. This means that governments usually cannot know who is exchanging bitcoins or for what purpose.

Bitcoin users can exchange bitcoins with each other one-on-one, without needing to rely on any intermediary. Once a price has been settled, bitcoins change possession digitally without the involvement of a bank. The new transaction is then verified and added into the public ledger, and everyone who holds a copy of the ledger receives the updated information. The bitcoin ledger is updated about once every ten minutes, so it can take that long or occasionally even longer for the transaction to go through.

Blockchains

Bitcoin and similar cryptocurrencies use something called blockchain technology to ensure the legitimacy and reliability of the system. A "block" is simply a bundle of bitcoin transactions in the form of a list. Blocks are verified, then added to a decentralized or distributed public ledger, or "blockchain."

Before a new block can be added to the blockchain, it must be given a "hash," a string of numbers and letters that looks random but is actually generated according to a set of rules. The hash must be generated from a combination of three different types of information:

- The transaction data in the block.

- The hash from the previous block in the blockchain.

- A random number called a "nonce."

These are then transformed into a new hash using an algorithm called SHA-256, and the hash is added to the end of the block. Anyone applying the same algorithm to the same information would get the exact same hash, but no one can tell just by looking at the hash what the information originally was.

Anyone who wanted to check the authenticity of the hash would only need to re-encrypt the block according to the same protocol. If the two hashes are the same, the blocks are the same. If the two hashes are different, something has been changed in one of the two blocks.

Because the hash also encrypts information about the previous block in the chain, any change to one block's hash would change the hash for all the other blocks that followed after it in the chain. This means that no one can change even a single number in a single transaction without changing the hash, which would then automatically change every hash in every block further down the chain. The result is that any attempt to commit fraud by changing a transaction would be noticed immediately and rejected by all the nodes, making it effectively impossible to interfere with the system.

In addition, anyone can examine the blockchain at any time and trace the legitimacy of every transaction back through the chain to the very first block, the "genesis block" first mined by Satoshi Nakamoto himself when he released the bitcoin software.

Blockchain technology was the big new idea that made bitcoin possible. Before the blockchain was invented, digital currencies depended on a trusted centralized authority to guarantee the validity of every transaction.

For example, every transaction includes a timestamp. If you tried to re-use the same unit of digital currency, the different timestamps would show that you had spent the same money twice at two different times. Unfortunately, the whole system depended on the trustworthiness of the authority in control of the timestamps.

Mining Bitcoins

The blockchain removes the need for a central authority by distributing the public ledger to all the different nodes at the same time. Any node can verify a transaction block and add it to the public ledger after generating a new hash for it, and all the nodes will then receive the updated ledger. Why is anyone willing to go to the trouble of verifying a transaction block, giving it a hash and adding it to the ledger? Because they get paid to do so!

Nodes are rewarded for verifying and updating the ledger in two different ways – they receive a transaction fee, and they are also awarded with brand-new bitcoins. Currently, the reward for adding a block stands at 12.5 bitcoins. However, the reward is automatically cut in half after every 210,000 blocks, which happens about once every four years. The reward will fall to zero once 21 million bitcoins are in circulation. This means that there are a finite number of bitcoins to "discover."

This is similar to the process of mining for gold or some other precious metal. Every time someone finds a piece of gold and digs it out of the earth, there is less gold for anyone else to discover in the future. At some point, all the gold in the ground will have been dug up and there won't be any more. The process for creating new bitcoins mimics the process of mining for precious metals, which is why it is known as "bitcoin mining."

Bitcoin Wallets

When you receive a bitcoin through mining or through any other type of transaction, it goes in a "wallet." Just as a bitcoin is not a physical piece of currency like a dollar bill or a coin, a bitcoin wallet is not a physical wallet. It is actually just a digital record of your bitcoins, tied to a set of encryption keys. One of these is your public bitcoin address, a string of numbers and letters people can use to send you bitcoins. The other is a private key that gives you access to your bitcoins.

If you lose your private encryption key, there is no way to access your bitcoins and they are gone forever. For this reason, people save their private keys using various methods, such as writing them down or storing them somewhere or even memorizing them. There are even novelty coins and paper wallets with bitcoin keys printed or embossed on them, but even though these may look like real coins or real wallets they are not. The private key is the important part, and it serves only to access your bitcoins over the internet. The actual bitcoins are not stored anywhere, they are simply part of the blockchain ledger.

There are several different types of bitcoin wallet. Hardware wallets are devices that securely store the keys needed to access your bitcoins. Hardware wallets are designed to be safe even when inserted into a computer infected by malware, which cannot access the keys.

Software wallets are more common, and again there are different types of software wallet. A "full client" contains the entire blockchain or a large chunk of it, so it takes up a lot of memory. A "lightweight wallet" communicates with a full client stored on another device, so it requires much less processing power. Lightweight wallets are used on smartphones and other devices without enough memory to run a full client.

Online wallets exist only on the internet, which can be convenient but also vulnerable. If you store your private keys in an online wallet, hackers could potentially get into the site, find your keys and steal all your bitcoins. This isn't likely to happen to you, but it is not impossible. One advantage of using an online wallet is that you can't lose it. If you store your bitcoin keys in a physical storage medium such as a paper wallet, losing the wallet means losing your bitcoins.

There is no way to access your bitcoins without the correct private key.

CHAPTER 2
THE EVOLUTION OF MONEY

Although bitcoin is often referred to as a cryptocurrency, not everyone agrees that it ought to be considered a currency at all. It certainly isn't a "fiat currency" – the type of currency issued on behalf of a government by a central bank. However, it does seem to fit the basic definition of money as a valuable object that is commonly accepted as payment for a good or service.

Human beings have used many different things as money, from cattle to gold to sacks of barley. If we limit our definition of "money" to currency issued by a nation state, we will leave out many of the forms money has actually taken throughout history.

History of Money

The Greek philosopher Aristotle thought that money was probably invented to replace a barter system. In a barter economy, people trade goods directly without any medium of exchange. The problem with a barter system is that you have to find someone who wants what you have and has what you want. This can obviously be cumbersome, so people invented money as a way to simplify the process.

A modern philosopher named David Graeber has argued that there is no historical evidence that a large-scale barter economy actually existed in premodern societies. There is much more evidence for the existence of gift economies, in which people regularly give each other gifts without a specific agreement to be paid back in kind. Because everyone in a gift economy is constantly giving and receiving gifts, people expect to get back roughly as much as they give. Graeber argues that this eventually evolved into an expectation that a specific person would give you a gift of a specific value, and that money was invented as a system of credit to facilitate this sort of exchange.

Whichever interpretation is the correct one, early money systems took many different forms. People used cattle or sacks of grain as money in many ancient societies. Some ancient societies used precious metals such as gold or silver. The main reason for using precious metals is that it is much easier to transport and store bars of metal than herds of cattle or sacks of grain. It is also much easier to subdivide them when needed. If an object costs half a bar of gold, it is easy enough to cut a gold bar in half – but what would you do if an object cost half a cow?

Subdividing bars of metal eventually evolved into minting coins, which allowed for smaller subdivisions of value based on the weight and purity of the metal in the coin. Carrying around huge quantities of gold or silver coins is still not very convenient, so merchants began to use "bills of exchange" in medieval times. A bill of exchange is simply a letter instructing someone to give the bearer a certain quantity of precious metal. A form of credit, the bill of exchange is clearly only a small step from paper currency.

True paper currency emerged in China during the Song Dynasty, and spread to Europe during the

Middle Ages. For a long time, money was mostly issued by private banks in the form of banknotes. A banknote represented a promise to give the bearer a certain amount of gold or some other precious metal on demand. Despite this fact, banks printed so many banknotes that they could never possibly have made good on them all.

Over time, national governments began to issue banknotes through their own centralized banks. Paper money finally became true "fiat currency," issued by government fiat through the government's own bank. Fiat currency existed alongside private banknotes for some time, but eventually fiat currency gained a near monopoly. This happened in England in 1694 when the Bank of England was given the right to issue all English banknotes, but didn't happen in the United States until the creation of the Federal Reserve in 1913.

The banknote was essentially a symbolic form of currency that did not really represent a specific amount of gold. If too many customers cashed in at once, the bank would immediately go under because it never really had that much gold on hand. Despite this fact, the US Dollar could still be exchanged directly for gold all over the world until 1971, when President Nixon abolished the practice. From that point onward, currency has been an entirely symbolic concept. When you deposit a thousand dollars in your local bank, you should not assume that the bank will actually store your thousand dollars in the vault in case you need it. Instead, your thousand dollars will be used for loans and investments. As with the banknote, if everyone went to the bank to withdraw their money at once, the bank would not have that much money available and it would collapse.

Much of the world's money now exists solely in digital form, and is exchanged between banks through the computer with no gold or paper currency ever changing hands. It's only a small step from this to the invention of cryptocurrency.

Digital Gold

In a sense, the bitcoin combines the modern concept of digital money with the old system in which a banknote represented a tangible good. Bitcoins are often referred to as "digital gold," because many aspects of the bitcoin system mimic the process of mining for gold. In effect, users who volunteer to verify the transactions of other users generate new bitcoins for their own use, just as if they were mining them. However, if gold was just lying around everywhere for anyone to pick up easily, it would not be worth anything. A new hash can be generated instantly using a software program designed for the purpose – just as easy as picking up gold lying around on the ground. If bitcoins could be generated from the transaction data alone, a bitcoin would be so easy to create that it would be worth almost nothing. In addition, all 21 million bitcoins would be generated very quickly and the supply would dry up.

To keep this from happening, the bitcoin protocol specifies a difficulty target. This means that the hash has to look a certain way. The only way to change the hash is to change one of the pieces of information used to generate it. You can't change the transaction data or the hash from the previous block, so how can you affect the hash? By changing the nonce, the random number included when generating the hash.

Bitcoin miners keep trying one nonce after another until they can produce a hash that meets the difficulty target. This is known as "proof of work," and it makes it much harder to create new bitcoins. Bitcoin miners use specialized computer systems to crunch the numbers and produce new hashes until they succeed in coming up with a hash that meets the difficulty target. The number of nonces that must be attempted to successfully create a hash is in the hundreds of quintillions. The first miner to do so gets credited with that block and earns the reward for adding it to the blockchain. The "proof of work" requirement is designed to mimic the difficulty of having to dig for gold rather than just picking it up from the ground.

In the early days of bitcoin, it was possible to mine for new bitcoins using a personal computer. The difficulty of bitcoin mining has steadily increased, and now requires a special computer system with enough processing power to find the right nonce faster than all its rivals.

As more people try their hands at bitcoin mining, more computers compete with each other to verify the blocks, find the right nonce, add the block to the blockchain and get paid. This tends to drive down the time in between the creation of new blocks, and could potentially destabilize the system by creating new bitcoins too quickly. To keep this from happening, the bitcoin protocol simply adjusts the difficulty target, making it harder and slower to find the right nonce. If it gets too hard and the system starts to slow down, the bitcoin protocol reduces the difficulty level.

This "target value" is adjusted once every 2016 blocks. This happens about once every two weeks. The goal is for each block to take about ten minutes to mine, so the difficulty level will be increased if the average has dropped below ten minutes and decreased if it has climbed above ten minutes.

Bitcoin vs Gold

Considering that the entire bitcoin system was designed to mimic the process of mining for gold, the obvious question is whether bitcoins are really anything like gold and which one is a better investment.

One reason people invest in gold is that you can count on gold to always be valuable. Even if the entire world economy collapsed in a huge depression or was destroyed by a new world war, gold would still be scarce and people would still want it. Severe economic crises can sometimes make paper currency almost worthless, but even though the price of gold can be volatile it is never worthless. Because of this, gold has traditionally been seen as a way to protect wealth from instability.

One huge difference between the two is that gold really exists in the physical world, while bitcoins do not. If some disaster causes all the world's computer records to disappear overnight, gold would almost certainly still be valuable but all the bitcoins would be gone.

On the other hand, this would only matter if you actually had physical possession of all your gold. Any gold you owned as an investment through the internet would also be gone. Most aspects of our financial systems are now virtual in much the same way as bitcoins are.

In less extreme situations, bitcoins do have some advantages over gold as a protection against instability. As long as you can access the internet, you can access your bitcoins, so you could carry a fortune in your wallet even if society was in upheaval all around you. That's not something you can do with gold.

Gold is valuable because it is scarce and because it isn't easy to acquire. Bitcoins are designed to be increasingly scarce – there will never be more than 21 million of them, and people are finding new bitcoins about once every ten minutes. Bitcoins are also hard to acquire, because you can't mine for bitcoins without the expensive computer systems needed to do so.

According to a 2014 article in *Fortune* magazine, bitcoin is actually superior to gold in this respect. Nobody knows exactly how much gold is out there to find, so even though it is a scarce and finite resource no one can say exactly how scarce or how finite it is. The scarcity of bitcoins is designed into the system, so we know exactly how scarce and how finite bitcoins are.

Gold can be confiscated by the government and it has been before. The US government made it illegal to own gold for a period of time during the Great Depression, and confiscated all the gold it could get its hands on. Bitcoin transactions are nearly anonymous, so you might think there's no way to confiscate bitcoins – but you'd be wrong. If the government gets access to your private key it controls your bitcoins, and it regularly does so when confiscating the assets of drug traffickers. Gold can be bought privately and then hidden, so it is arguably safer from being confiscated although hiding it in such a situation would obviously be illegal.

There is no simple answer to the question of whether gold or bitcoin is a safer investment. The decision to invest in one or the other must be based on your individual goals and circumstances.

ALFORD BENSON

CHAPTER 3
USING BITCOINS

Millions of people use bitcoins to pay for goods and services, and more than 100,000 businesses accept bitcoins as payment. Bitcoin mining may be an activity for the few, but anyone can use bitcoins to buy and sell things.

The first known purchase involving bitcoins happened in 2010, when the bitcoin project was still seen as an experiment and individual bitcoins were worth almost nothing. A bitcoin miner named Laszlo Hanyecz offered 10,000 bitcoins to anyone who would order two pizzas and have them delivered to his house. Hanyecz got his pizza, and those 10,000 bitcoins are now worth around $25 million USD.

To make a purchase with bitcoins, all you need to do is to send your bitcoins to the seller's bitcoin address. To accept a payment from someone else, all you need to do is to send them your bitcoin address. It's as simple as sending or receiving an email. You can send and receive bitcoins with an app on your smartphone, which makes the entire process extremely simple. A bitcoin address can also be presented in the form of a QR-code, which can be scanned much like a barcode.

It doesn't cost anything to receive bitcoins from someone else, but you might need to pay a fee when sending bitcoins. The fee is an incentive to bitcoin miners to process your transaction, so the higher the fee the more likely they will process it quickly. You can always decide for yourself how much to send – it is impossible for anyone to add any charges to your payment.

Considering that a single bitcoin is now worth around $12,000 USD, you may wonder how can you purchase anything that costs less than that. The answer is that bitcoins can be divided up into smaller units just like other forms of currency. In the case of bitcoins, these units are simply fractions of a single bitcoin:

- The satoshi is the smallest unit, at 0.00000001 bitcoins.

- A microbitcoin is 0.000001 bitcoins.

- A millie, millibit or millibitcoin is 0.001 bitcoins, approximately $12.

Bitcoin Safety

Keeping your bitcoins safe is just as important as keeping cash or other valuables safe. If a hacker succeeds in emptying out your bitcoin wallet, there is nothing you can do – those bitcoins are gone. If you keep your credentials offline and then lose or forget them, those bitcoins are gone.

Many people use online bitcoin wallets for ease and convenience, but online wallet services have been hacked before and certainly will be hacked again. To make it harder for a hacker to target your online wallet, use two-factor authentication (requiring two different forms of identification, such as a password and a separate contact email). Bitcoin.org also recommends keeping only a portion of your bitcoins in your online wallet and leaving the majority of your bitcoin savings in "cold storage." This means saving your private key in some form that cannot possibly be hacked because it is offline in the first place – for instance, by memorizing it or writing it down somewhere.

Because you can lose all your bitcoins if you lose your keys, bitcoin.org also recommends backing up all your wallet information. For instance, if you store your keys on a computer hard-drive you could also have them on a separate flash drive. Of course, anyone who stole the backup could get access to your keys, so you should also download encryption software and use it to encrypt all your backups.

Even if you have done everything possible to protect your wallet from unauthorized access, you can still lose your bitcoins to a clever scam. If you send bitcoins to someone in payment for a product, there is no way to retrieve the bitcoins if they refuse to send the product. Unlike a check or a credit card transaction, you cannot cancel a payment once you have made it. Approach all bitcoin transactions with the same caution you would use if sending cash.

Bitcoin Transaction Security

The security of the bitcoin network is not guaranteed by any central authority, but by the transparency of the system itself. The entire blockchain ledger is publicly available, and the software that runs the system has always been open source. This means that anyone can examine the code and verify that the system does exactly what it is supposed to do, and that no one is manipulating it or controlling it in any way.

If the bitcoin system was under the control of a central authority, your ability to trust the system would depend on your trust of that authority. Because the system is neutral and transparent, you don't have to trust anyone – you can check for yourself whenever you want.

In a transaction involving credit cards, checks or Paypal, the person making the payment can cancel it and void the transaction. This creates many opportunities for fraud that simply don't exist with bitcoin. A bitcoin payment cannot be cancelled or called back once it has been made.

However, you do need to be aware of this whenever you make a bitcoin payment. As soon as you hit "send," the funds are gone for all practical purposes. If something goes wrong, you can ask the person you made the payment to if they would be willing to return the funds – but there's probably nothing you can do if they refuse.

It's not technically impossible for a bitcoin transaction to be canceled, but it is extremely unlikely after the transaction has been confirmed and added to the blockchain. The possibility of a double-spending fraud does exist up until that happens.

When someone sends you bitcoins and they appear in your wallet, it is technically possible for them to spend the same bitcoins somewhere else until the original transaction is confirmed. In theory, the bitcoin nodes should spot the double transaction and reject it, but it is possible that a node would verify the wrong transaction by mistake. If the fraudulent transaction offered a higher processing fee, it is even possible that the miner would knowingly accept the fraudulent transaction to earn the fee. This issue was first pointed out by a bitcoin developer named Peter

Todd, who argued that bitcoin had not completely solved the double spending problem. If you wait until the transaction is confirmed to take any further action, you should be safe from this potential issue. Just remember – bitcoin transactions are secure once they're in the blockchain, but not before that.

ALFORD BENSON

CHAPTER 4
THE BITCOIN BLACK MARKET

Is bitcoin the currency of choice for criminals? That's certainly one of the stereotypes about cryptocurrency, thanks in part to the notorious "Silk Road" website. The original silk road was an ancient network of trading routes between Europe and Asia. For many centuries, merchant caravans trekked across the silk road carrying silk, exotic spices and many other products across vast distances. Silk Road founder Ross William Ulbricht used this image of adventure across exotic trade routes to promote his website as an internet black market, operating on the dark web through the anonymous Tor browser.

The "dark web" is a term for hidden websites that cannot be found on any standard search engine. To find a site on the dark web, you have to know where to look for it. For example, the original dark web address of the Silk Road was *tydgccykixpbu6uz.onion.* Obviously, that isn't an address that would show up in a casual search.

Because many sites on the dark web are illegal or controversial in one way or another, most users access these sites only through browsers, such as Tor, that disguise the identity and location of the user.

Many people associate bitcoin with the Silk Road because the site was one of the first to accept bitcoins as payment. For the drug dealers and users doing business on the Silk Road, the apparent anonymity of bitcoins seemed like the perfect way to complete a transaction without getting caught. Neither the purchaser nor the seller would ever know each other's true identity, so in theory there was no way to get in trouble.

Theory and reality don't always match. Ulbricht disguised his own identity by using the pseudonym "Dread Pirate Roberts," and his assistants used pseudonyms like "Variety Jones," and "Smedley." Ulbricht and his co-conspirators claimed to have created the site out of libertarian idealism, a viewpoint also shared by many bitcoin enthusiasts. However, Ulbricht actually operated more like a traditional gangster than he let on – he is alleged to have attempted to arrange several contract killings, apparently without success.

Ulbricht's identity as the Dread Pirate Roberts was unmasked by the FBI, which may have used advanced hacking techniques to trick the site into revealing its real IP address. Ulbricht was arrested, prosecuted and sentenced to life in prison without parole. The site has since been restored and taken down several times, and other administrators have been caught and prosecuted. The Federal government typically seizes the assets of arrested drug traffickers, and it has acquired so many bitcoins through this process that it has had to auction them off in large quantities.

Shutting down the Silk Road for good has not been easy – would-be kingpins keep setting up new versions of it no matter how many times the FBI takes it down. At this point it may no longer matter much anyway. The dark web is now filled with other black-market sites that accept bitcoin or other cryptocurrencies for everything from drugs to weapons to computer viruses.

Some of these services have turned out to be nothing but huge scams for stealing bitcoins. Darknet markets often use an escrow system, in which they have temporary possession of user's bitcoins before passing them on to the receiver. In 2014, a highly-regarded darknet market called Evolution shut down without warning "for maintenance." Users eventually figured out that Evolution's reputation for trustworthiness and customer service had all been part of the scam, allowing it to amass bitcoins worth $12 million USD in escrow and then disappear with it all.

Bizarrely enough, Ulbricht was alleged to have fallen for a bitcoin scam himself. When a Silk Road administrator named Curtis Clark Green was caught for drug dealing and prosecuted, the FBI claims that Ubricht tried to have him killed by a hit man to keep him quiet. The hit man was really a Federal agent, who simply pretended to have done the hit and kept the payment. For some unknown reason, Ulbricht was never charged with attempted murder, but the accusations did play a role in his life sentence upon conviction for running the Silk Road. Two of the agents involved in the case – one from the DEA and one from the Secret Service – were later convicted and imprisoned for extorting bitcoins from Ulbricht.

Is Bitcoin Anonymous?

At the height of the Silk Road, bitcoin was so closely associated with the dark web in many people's minds that it was assumed the cryptocurrency could not survive the crackdown. Before the original Silk Road was shut down, between 4.5 and 9% of all bitcoin transactions were conducted through the Silk Road website.

That's about 1.35 million bitcoins, an unbelievably huge figure given what bitcoins are now worth. However, the predictions of gloom and doom turned out not to be accurate, because many people use bitcoins without ever visiting the dark web or browsing a darknet market at all. Still, it is obviously the case that cryptocurrency appeals to criminals – most likely because they feel anonymous using it despite all the people who have already been caught and prosecuted.

This raises the obvious question – is bitcoin anonymous, and if so then how do people keep getting caught when using it for criminal purposes?

The simple fact is that bitcoin is not anonymous. Nobody can tell who was involved in a particular transaction just by looking at the blockchain, but that doesn't mean there's no way to figure it out. For instance, many bitcoin-related services require personal information during the sign-up process. If you sign up for any of these services with your real personal information, that means there's a record connecting you to your public bitcoin address. If you have a bitcoin wallet on your smartphone or your personal computer, transaction in the blockchain can be traced back to you with surprising ease.

Because the blockchain is publicly available for anyone to look at, the FBI can examine it without a warrant or subpoena. In the Silk Road case, they were able to compare the transactions listed in the blockchain with the bitcoin wallet on Ross Ulbricht's personal computer. This proved beyond a reasonable doubt that Ulbricht had received 700,254 bitcoins directly from the Silk

Road, an $18 million-dollar fortune. Ulbricht's mistaken belief in bitcoin's anonymity left him more vulnerable than if he had used a traditional bank – because of the transparency of the blockchain, Ulbricht might as well have been paying himself in marked bills!

The bitcoin address is effectively a pseudonym, disguising your real identity but not erasing all trace of it. That's why bitcoin is often described as "pseudo-anonymous" – it's anonymous enough for basic privacy, but not enough to keep your career as an international drug lord secret forever. Aside from the moral issues of engaging in criminal activity, relying on bitcoin and Tor alone will not make it safe to be a professional criminal. In some ways, it actually makes prosecution easier.

Ultimately, criminals are interested in money and bitcoin is a form of money so it is used by criminals. There is nothing inherently criminal about bitcoin itself, and investing in bitcoins will not make you a shady character if you aren't one already. You can buy and sell bitcoins all you like without any worries about the government, but not if you are using your bitcoins to buy or sell illegal things – just like with any other form of money.

Having said that, bitcoin was designed with privacy in mind, and there are legitimate reasons for wanting to do business anonymously. There are ways to further obscure your identity when using bitcoin.

For instance, you can purchase a "burner" phone that isn't registered in your name, set up a bitcoin wallet, and then buy bitcoins locally with cash. The idea is to meet in a public place, hand over the right amount of cash, and have the seller send the bitcoins to the wallet on your burner phone. The potential risks of meeting a stranger with cash in hand should be obvious, but the bitcoins in that particular wallet would then be very difficult to trace to you. Bitcoin ATMs also allow you to purchase bitcoins with cash, and could theoretically be used to acquire bitcoins anonymously as long as your bitcoin wallet could not be linked to your identity in some other way.

No matter what steps you take, there's no realistic way to guarantee that authorities will not discover your identity if you're engaged in illegal activities. Not only were the Silk Road administrators identified and prosecuted, but a number of the drug dealers using the Silk Road to sell their products were caught as well. In the final analysis, the idea that bitcoin is the perfect currency for criminals is a stereotype at best and delusional at worst.

ALFORD BENSON

CHAPTER 5
PITFALLS AND VULNERABILITIES

Bitcoin offers many advantages over other forms of currency, but it does come with some disadvantages. Some of these disadvantages will probably disappear or at least decrease as bitcoin becomes more widely used and better understood.

One disadvantage of the bitcoin market is volatility. The value of the bitcoin has been known to fluctuate wildly, largely because the number of people who use bitcoin is still relatively small compared to the number of people who use traditional currencies. So many people use the US dollar that a single trade can have only a limited effect on the value of the dollar as a whole. Not so with bitcoins, the value of which can be affected by the actions of a smaller number of users.

The volatility of the bitcoin market also affects the currency's fungibility, meaning the ability to be sure that one bitcoin will always be worth the same as another bitcoin. To give one example, if you make a purchase for $15 USD and then decide to return it, you would expect to get back exactly $15 USD. A dollar is a dollar, after all.

If you make a purchase for 15 BTC (or fifteen bitcoins) and then the market surges, those 15 bitcoins could suddenly be worth a lot more. Assuming you were dealing with a merchant willing to accept returns on items purchased with bitcoins, can you really expect the merchant to return a sum worth much more than what you actually spent? It might seem unfair, but unless a bitcoin is always treated as equivalent to another bitcoin regardless of circumstances, then the currency has no fungibility and thus lacks a major characteristic of fiat currency.

Some bitcoin users have also suggested blacklisting bitcoin addresses known to be stolen or involved in criminal activity. This sounds like a common-sense way to discourage fraud, but it would also have the effect of destroying bitcoin's fungibility because of the transparency of the blockchain. Imagine trying to spend some bitcoins only to find out that they were stolen at some point before you acquired them and have now been blacklisted. Through no fault of your own, you would have purchased worthless bitcoins.

Another disadvantage is that bitcoin is not yet as widely accepted as fiat currency. Many vendors accept bitcoins but many more do not. With any new technology, users benefit from something called the 'network effect" every time a new person decides to use the technology. For example, if only one person owns a telephone, that telephone is useless. If a few people own telephones, each telephone is at least a little bit useful. If many people own telephones it becomes convenient to everyone, and once enough people own a telephone it becomes an essential item. Bitcoin is still in the early stages of this process, and most merchants do not yet feel that it is essential to accept bitcoins.

Bitcoin is still in "beta" mode, meaning that not every aspect of the system is fully designed and functional to the level that it could be. Bitcoin developers are tweaking the code, developing new apps and figuring out what features bitcoin users are going to need as the currency becomes more popular. Until this process is a bit further along, you may find that existing services are not yet capable of doing exactly what you need with bitcoins.

Another possible concern is that the blockchain will run into size limitations. Satoshi Nakamoto designed the bitcoin software to reject any block larger than 1 MB. This was intended as an anti-hacking feature, but what about huge transactions that could be too large to fit into a single block?

An inconsistent regulatory environment is another concern. Bitcoin businesses in Montana and New Mexico are much less heavily regulated than those in New York or California. Of course, this issue is hardly unique to bitcoin.

Many of these issues should resolve themselves over time, as more people use bitcoin and more merchants accept it. Regulations will also probably stabilize as governments figure out what to do with this new market.

Vulnerabilities in Bitcoin Exchange

Although many people have used and continue to use bitcoin exchanges, their history has been rather checkered and the security of this type of service is far from guaranteed. As the Bitcoin.org website warns, "Many exchanges... suffered from security breaches in the past and such services generally still do not provide enough insurance and security".

One of the first and (for a time) most successful bitcoin exchanges was called Mt. Gox, short for "Magic the Gathering Currency Exchange" because it was originally designed for enthusiasts of the card game before its founder realized bitcoin would be more a more profitable business. At the height of Mt. Gox's success in 2013-2014, more than 70% of all transactions involving bitcoin were being conducted through Mt. Gox.

The company began to run into serious problems long before that. In 2011, a computer hacker using stolen credentials temporarily succeeded in transferring so many bitcoins to his own wallet that the value of a bitcoin dropped to just one penny. The bitcoin system's self-correcting features came to the rescue in this instance, and the fraudulent transaction was rejected within minutes. Mt. Gox was able to prove that it had regained control by announcing a transaction ahead of time and then carrying it out as promised, and the bitcoin market stabilized with confidence restored. Later that same year, 2609 BTC were sent to invalid bitcoin addresses due to an error in the Mt. Gox exchange, causing them to become permanently irretrievable.

In 2013, the entire blockchain temporarily split in two, with two separate and incompatible logs. Mt. Gox suspended trading, causing a 23% drop in bitcoin's value. As with previous issues, the matter was resolved quickly and bitcoin recovered its value in just a few hours. A bitcoin was worth around $48 at that time, but the market for bitcoin suddenly began to grow very rapidly and the price shot up so fast that Mt. Gox suspended trading again in April 2013 to try to slow things down a little.

After trading was resumed, the value of a bitcoin stabilized at around $100 for a time. In May of 2013, the Department of Homeland Security accused Mt. Gox's U.S. subsidiary of operating an unregistered exchange. Several bitcoin exchanges have run into the same problem and been forced to shut down, and some company officials have even been sent to prison for running currency exchanges without the necessary licenses.

Mt. Gox attempted to get the issue resolved with the U.S. government, but the company's legal troubles resulted in increasingly long delays. Customers often couldn't withdraw their bitcoins for weeks or even months at a stretch. In 2014, Mt. Gox suspended all withdrawals and took a closer look at its financial situation.

What it found was a disaster – around 850,000 bitcoins had somehow gone missing. 100,000 of these belonged to the company, but 750,000 belonged to Mt. Gox customers. The Mt. Gox website went down and the company filed for bankruptcy while trying to find the missing bitcoins. About 200,000 were found in an unused company bitcoin wallet, but the other 650,000 were most likely stolen by hackers. The hackers had apparently been raiding Mt. Gox's online bitcoin wallet since 2011 without anyone noticing what was going on.

In 2015, Mt. Gox CEO Mark Karpelès was arrested in Japan and charged with embezzlement and fraud. The bitcoins he was accused of stealing were not the same as the missing bitcoins, which would now be worth about $1.625 billion USD.

After the fall of Mt. Gox, Bitfinex became the dominant bitcoin exchange company, which it remains as of this writing. In 2016, Bitfinex lost 119,756 customer bitcoins in another hack, showing that the security of bitcoin exchange is still far from established.

Protect Yourself

Hackers can only target a wallet that is connected to the internet. The 650,000 stolen Mt. Gox bitcoins all came out of the company's own hot wallet, and could not have been stolen if they were not stored in this way. How can bitcoins be stored off the internet when they only exist on the internet in the first place?

That's a very good question, but the answer is surprisingly simple. Bitcoins actually exist only within the blockchain ledger. No wallet, whether online or offline actually stores any bitcoins – only the information needed to access and use them. If you store this information in a hot wallet, hackers can potentially access it. If you keep the information in cold storage, there's no way they can do that.

There are a number of different ways to put your bitcoins in cold storage. One of the cleverest systems is to set up two computers, one connected to the internet and one offline. The online computer has a "watching wallet," allowed to create transactions but not to sign them with your private key. The offline computer has the private key. When you need to transfer funds from cold storage, you create the transaction form online and then download to a USB drive. Then you plug the USB drive into the offline computer to add your key to the form, before plugging it back into the online computer to complete the transaction. Other options include using a hardware wallet or paper wallet to store your keys so they remain offline.

The simplest way to keep your bitcoins in cold storage is to write them down and not store them on any other media at all, but of course there's always the risk that you could lose the paper.

There is also at least a slight risk that a thief could find the paper, recognize the string of letters and numbers as a bitcoin address, and steal all your bitcoins. To protect against this possibility, don't write down the public key and the private key on the same piece of paper.

Cold storage is obviously a bit cumbersome, so Bitcoin.org advises keeping a small amount of bitcoins in your hot wallet for minor purchases. This way you only risk losing a small amount to hackers, but you still have the convenience of using bitcoin easily. Many people, even major players in the bitcoin world, have kept huge amounts of bitcoin in a hot wallet and then lost it all to hackers.

CHAPTER 6
BITCOIN EXCHANGE

Bitcoin exchanges are online services that make it easy for the average investor to buy and sell bitcoins. Although Mt. Gox once had a virtual monopoly on this market, its collapse has opened up the field and there are now a number of different bitcoin exchanges out there. Although bitcoin exchanges have a checkered history, many of the current exchanges have introduced strong new security features to avoid a repeat of the Mt. Gox disaster. For instance, Mt. Gox made the nearly unbelievable mistake of storing both its own funds and those of its customers in hot storage, leaving vast amounts of money vulnerable to hackers. When you're considering a bitcoin exchange, look for companies that keep all funds in cold storage – or better yet, cold storage protected by additional features such as strong encryption.

You might also want to check on the company's legal status. A company that is fully licensed and legally compliant may not offer as much privacy as a company that isn't, but at least you won't have to worry that the CEO will suddenly be indicted!

How Bitcoin Exchanges Work

The basic structure of a bitcoin exchange is something like a traditional bank. You set up an account with the exchange, deposit money into your account, and then use that money to buy bitcoins. You can also sell any bitcoins you have to other users, and you can withdraw your money from the exchange much like a bank. Withdrawing your money can be a little slower or more complicated than withdrawing from a bank, depending on exactly what you are trying to do and on which exchange you are using. For instance, if you want to be able to turn your bitcoins into dollar bills and take them out from an ATM, there's a process you have to go through first and it is not instant. If you just want to transfer your bitcoins to a private wallet, you should be able to do that more or less instantly.

Bitcoin exchanges don't just deal in bitcoins. Customers buying and selling bitcoins use other forms of currency, including other forms of cryptocurrency. Bitcoin exchanges typically accept several different major currencies, such as the United States dollar, the Japanese yen, the Euro, the British pound and the Russian ruble. You may also be able to use digital gold currency such as Pecunix, which is digital (like bitcoin) but based on a gold standard (like the US dollar used to be). The exchange will usually accept payment by money order, wire transfer or credit card, and some exchanges offer prepaid cards that make it possible to withdraw your balance anonymously from a standard ATM.

The bitcoin exchange protects you from one of the potential pitfalls of using bitcoins – the risk that a dishonest vendor will receive your payment but then refuse to send the product. Bitcoin exchanges generally provide guarantees against this sort of risk. On the other hand, you do have to trust the stability and security of the exchange itself – and as we have seen, this has sometimes been an issue. One reason to use a bitcoin exchange that is properly licensed and regulated is that the owners of the exchange have shown their interest in staying on the right side of the law. This would have to be considered a good sign when it comes to trusting them with your money!

When you want to buy bitcoins on a bitcoin exchange, you place a "bid" or "buy order" offering to buy bitcoins and listing the maximum price you are willing to pay. When you want to sell bitcoins, you place an "ask" or "sell order" offering to sell bitcoins and listing the minimum price you are willing to sell them for. The rate at which people are buying and selling bitcoins determines the value of the currency at any given time. If no one is willing to buy a bitcoin for $12,000 but people are willing to buy for $11,000, the value of a bitcoin drops to $11,000. As with any other type of investment, the goal is obviously to buy for a lower price and sell for a higher price.

Comparing Bitcoin Exchanges

Every bitcoin exchange works a little bit differently, with different options and different rules. To give one example, trading on the CEX.IO exchange works like this:

- Set up an account using your email and a strong password. If you'd prefer for your bitcoin activity to remain private, use an email address you don't use in any other context.

- Deposit money into your new account in dollars, rubles, euros or some other currency.

- Once the site credits you for the deposit and adjusts your balance, you can start buying bitcoins from other users through the site.

- Once you have some bitcoins, you can leave them in your CEX.IO account if you prefer. The site keeps the keys needed to access customer funds in encrypted cold storage, so this should be relatively safe. If you want to keep trading bitcoins, you can offer yours for sale. You can also withdraw your bitcoins by transferring them to a private wallet off the site.

- You don't have to have enough money to buy a whole bitcoin. At the time of writing, you could buy .008250 BTC for $100 USD, .016440 BTC for $200 USD, .041250 BTC for $500 USD or .082500 BTC for $1000 USD.

- The CEX.IO exchange supports credit cards and bank transfers, but recommends bank transfers for larger purchases. Customers making larger purchases can also upgrade to a business or corporate account to qualify for priority treatment.

- Customers can add any number of credit cards to their CEX.IO account, and the site is designed to allow you to buy bitcoins with just a few clicks.

- The site charges trading fees from 0.1 to 7%.

- CEX.IO also offers the option of automated bitcoin trading.

For comparison, this is how another bitcoin exchange called Coinbase works:

- New users must fill out an online form to set up an account similar to CEX.IO

- The exchange accepts international wire transfers, Technocash and several different types of digital currency including Litecoin and Ethereum.

- You'll need to complete some verification steps before you can use the account and there are four verification levels. The first three levels take only a couple of minutes. The fourth level can take a bit longer, usually a few days. Completion of each level increases user's weekly buy and sell limits.

- The site lists the current trading value of bitcoin, as well as the most recent price for which bitcoins have sold on the site, recent high and low prices and the trading volume.

- You can enter the amount of bitcoin you would like to sell on the site's front page.

- The site offers instant exchange of bitcoins.

- Coinbase is the largest Bitcoin storing company in the world. It holds over 600,000 customer wallets, and it's integrated into the US banking system.

- You can also access Coinbase exchange through the mobile app for iOS and Android, which is probably the best Bitcoin exchange apps on the market today.

This comparison is only illustrative, bitcoin exchanges are constantly adapting to stay ahead of the competition. When selecting a bitcoin exchange is important you consider factors such as ease of use, security policies and whether the exchange facilitates the type of trading you would like to do.

Market Orders, Limit Orders and Open Orders

The "open book" is the list of current buy or sell orders on a bitcoin exchange. If your order is available to be filled, it is called an "open order." If your order has been completed, it is closed and taken off the open book.

You have two basic options when trading bitcoins. If you just want to buy or sell some bitcoins immediately, you can make a market order. A market order will go through right away at the best price you can get at that moment.

However, that may not be the most effective approach if you're trying to make money by trading bitcoins. If you want to get a specific price, you should place a limit order. This specifies the price you are willing to pay for bitcoins or the price at which you are willing to sell your bitcoins. A limit order won't complete until someone agrees to the price you're proposing.

If no one seems interested in completing your limit order, check the current average price. If you're asking for too much compared to the average price, you may have to either change your order or wait longer to complete it. In some cases, an order may be "partially matched" before it is completed, in which case it remains on the order book.

In the most basic terms, a private investor trading in bitcoin would most likely use some variation on the following strategy:

- Find bitcoin at an unusually cheap price, by setting a limit order lower than the current average but within the range of recent transactions.

- Wait patiently until someone offers to sell at this price – most likely because they need to raise some cash quickly and cannot afford to wait for a better offer!

- Sell the same bitcoin for a higher price, either because the value of bitcoin goes up or because someone is willing to pay a higher price to acquire bitcoin immediately.

Of course, there is never going to be any guarantee that the value of bitcoins will go up instead of down. That depends on the market, and the bitcoin market can sometimes be volatile.

Restrictions and Regulations

Bitcoin exchange operators have been arrested and convicted on occasion for running unlicensed currency exchanges, which is one reason many of them operate from countries with fewer regulatory requirements. Others are in the process of getting all the licenses they need to become legally compliant, or in some cases they may already be properly licensed.

When a bitcoin exchange is compliant or is trying to become so, you will probably have to provide a lot more personal information before you can do business on the exchange. For example, btcmarkets.net requires passport or driver's license information so they can verify your identity, a process which may take several days. The site also bans all illegal activity, and you'd be foolish to use it for that purpose considering the amount of personal information they require from users.

Btcmarkets.net also forbids users from making ransomware payments through the site. Ransomware is a type of malicious software that encrypts your personal files. You can only get them unencrypted by making a ransom payment to the criminals using the software, usually in the form of bitcoins – but not through this particular exchange!

ALFORD BENSON

CHAPTER 7
BITCOIN INVESTING

The most obvious way to invest in bitcoin is simply to buy some, hoping to sell it later at a higher price. This approach does not require you to know much about investing or to place your trust in a money manager, but it does require you to set up your own wallet and handle the process yourself. In the early days of bitcoin, people would trade them almost on a whim – as in the famous case of the bitcoin pizza order. Those days are done!

Anyone who bought bitcoin early on, when it was worth almost nothing, has now realized an astronomical return on their initial investment. Bitcoins were worth only eight cents in July 2010, one dollar in February 2011, $100 in June 2013 and somewhere between $800 and $1150 at the start of 2017. Current prices are around $12,000 per bitcoin, so if you bought 100 bitcoins for a total of eight dollars back in 2010, you would now have $1,200,000 worth of bitcoins.

Returns like that are no longer to be expected, but many people are still getting involved in bitcoin for the first time. If bitcoin ends up replacing fiat currency the way its most optimistic proponents insist it will, then buying some today is still likely to pay off big in the future. If the entire bitcoin phenomenon is a bubble as its most pessimistic detractors insist, then the value of bitcoins will someday go tumbling down for good. It's a speculative investment, with big risks and the potential for big rewards. Even if you don't buy in to the utopian dreams of the bitcoin fanatics, there is still good reason to think you could make a profit by investing in bitcoins.

If you're interested in bitcoin but not ready to dive in and start speculating on bitcoin prices yourself, there are other ways to invest in bitcoin's future. Some of these are designed to mimic more traditional investments – a comforting option for someone new to bitcoin. You can buy shares in a bitcoin fund in exactly the same way you would buy shares in a traditional investment fund.

Investment Funds

Investors now have the option of investing in a fund that pools their bitcoins, allowing them to make profits through a wide variety of other investments. An investment fund combines the money provided by numerous investors to make much larger investments than any of them could ever make on their own. Traditional investment funds use fiat currencies for this purpose, investing in stocks, bonds and other financial instruments. Bitcoin investment funds work the exact same way, but they use bitcoins rather than a fiat currency.

Every investment fund has a prospectus, a document listing the goals of that particular fund. The money manager who runs the fund will make strategic decisions about how to invest the money in order to make a profit for the fund's investors. For example, Bitcoin Investment Bank uses a strategy called "double exponential moving average," designed to adapt quickly to sudden changes in the market.

This process can also be partially automated. For instance, the Bitcoin Investment Bank uses a bot (a software that performs an automated task) called the BIB Automatic Trading bot to run investment decisions for individual investors. The bot can invest in both traditional financial instruments and cryptocurrency markets, using bitcoin in both cases. Although the bot makes investing decisions automatically, it is overseen by human analysts. The analysts retain the ability to change investing strategies based on circumstances, so the process is not exclusively automatic.

You can also make a profit in bitcoins through arbitrage trading. Arbitrage refers to buying an asset in a market with a lower price and selling it in a different market that happens to have a higher price at that time. Bitcoin arbitrage trading can also be handled by your bitcoin investment fund.

The first bitcoin investment fund to be publicly listed and traded with full regulatory approval was the BIT or Bitcoin Investment Trust, established by Grayscale Industries in 2013. The BIT allows investors to purchase shares, making it possible to invest in bitcoin without personally buying and selling bitcoins. This can be a good option for investors who want to get in on the bitcoin market without having to set up a wallet and buy bitcoins themselves. As of this writing, each share in the BIT was worth 0.09273259 BTC.

Transaction Fees

If you're buying and selling bitcoin directly, you will probably have to pay a transaction fee. Transaction fees are used to motivate bitcoin miners to quickly process your transaction. If you're making a private transaction, you set the fee yourself. There's no rule that says you have to include a fee at all – but there's a catch.

If you decide not to include a fee, there's no reason for any bitcoin miner to include your transaction in a new block and get it added to the blockchain. Early on, the reward for mining a new block was high enough that many miners were willing to include some transactions without fees attached – just to put a new block together quickly and earn the reward. This is no longer the case, because the reward is automatically cut by 50% every 210,000 blocks. Miners depend more on transaction fees now, so they are no longer willing to include transactions without a fee.

The amount of the transaction fee typically depends on the current size of the "mempool," the list of transactions that have not yet been confirmed. When the mempool becomes unwieldy and transactions start taking longer and longer to confirm, people start offering larger and larger fees to motivate miners to prioritize their transaction. When the mempool becomes smaller, it is possible to get your transaction confirmed with a very small fee.

Between May and June 2017, the mempool became very large and transactions were not clearing quickly. In some cases, large numbers of transactions were still waiting to be confirmed days after they were originally made. In that kind of situation, the only way to be sure your transaction will clear quickly is to offer the biggest fee you can afford.

When the mempool dropped from 120 GB to 20 GB, transaction fees plummeted – one user reported sending $2,000 worth of bitcoins with only a 25-cent transaction fee, and having the transaction confirmed in just six minutes. In general, users are paying fees of one dollar or less as of this writing.

If you invest through a bitcoin investment fund, there are additional fees to consider. Investment funds may charge a "benchmark fee," payable when you meet your investment goals. Grayscale's Bitcoin Investment Trust charges an annual fee of 2%. Bitcoin Investment Bank charges trading fees starting at 0.0005 BTC.

Funds may also charge fees to withdraw your bitcoins.

Regulations

Because bitcoins are so new, the regulations affecting bitcoins are constantly changing and can be wildly different from place to place. Bitcoin is legal to use in the most jurisdictions around the world, but completely illegal in Bolivia, Ecuador, Kyrgyzstan and Bangladesh.

In the United States, different branches of the government seem to look at bitcoin differently. To the U.S. Treasury, bitcoin is a "convertible decentralized virtual currency". To the Commodity Futures Trading Commission, bitcoins are not a currency at all but a commodity. To the IRS, bitcoins are a type of property. To at least one U.S. judge, bitcoins are "funds."

Different U.S. states regulate bitcoins differently. The State of New York has a complete set of bitcoin regulations, requiring companies to issue receipts for all transactions, establish complaint policies, follow cybersecurity standards, introduce protections against money laundering, issue risk disclosure statements and employ compliance officers.

If you have any questions about bitcoin regulations, consult the security and exchange authorities in your jurisdiction.

Taxes

Bitcoin income can be taxed just like anything else, and taxes will vary from one jurisdiction to another just as regulations will. In Europe and the United Kingdom, bitcoin transactions are not subject to VAT, but they are subject to the equivalent GST tax in Australia.

As a general guideline, any income from bitcoins should be treated as self-employment income, which means that you will have to pay the self-employment tax but you can deduct your losses and business expenses. Many bitcoin speculators don't realize they can deduct any losses, and end up paying higher taxes than they actually need to despite having lost money on their bitcoin transactions.

The IRS considers bitcoins to be capital assets, which means that any profits from trading bitcoins are subject to the capital gains tax. (However, some countries don't have a capital gains tax at all, so if they apply the same logic then they would not be able to tax bitcoin profits.) The IRS treats bitcoins earned through mining as income, based on the value of the mined bitcoins on the day they were mined.

Consult a tax professional for advice on how to handle taxes on your bitcoin income. Some tax questions involving bitcoin are highly complicated, and different interpretations could yield different results that may or may not be accepted by the IRS when you go to file. Better to let a professional handle it!

ALFORD BENSON

CHAPTER 8
INVESTMENT RISKS

One concern you may have about investing in bitcoin is that the cryptocurrency has a history of price volatility. Yes, a single bitcoin is worth about $12,000 today – but what if it's worth a lot less than that tomorrow?

Price Volatility

There is some reason for these concerns, but understanding the causes of previous price crashes may help you avoid similar losses if you decide to invest in bitcoin. Bitcoins were originally traded on an internet forum called "bitcointalk,' where the famous offer to buy pizza with bitcoins was first made and accepted. Bitcoins had essentially no value in those early years, but once people started making real purchases with bitcoins interest in cryptocurrency began increasing rapidly.

In April 2010, BitcoinMarket.com became the first bitcoin exchange. Bitcoins at that time were worth about three cents. By May 2010, when the pizza order was placed, bitcoins were worth less than a single penny, but went back up to eight cents by July and were equivalent in value to the US dollar by February 2011. By early July of that year, the value of a bitcoin had soared to $31, but this turned out to be an investment bubble and the price of bitcoin dropped all the way back down to two dollars.

Bubbles are driven by over-enthusiasm, so any sudden surge in the value of bitcoin should probably be viewed with some caution. From 2011 to 2012 the price rose again bit by bit, reaching $13 in December. As of 2012, there were more than a thousand merchants who accepted bitcoins through the BitPay payment processor, so there was increasing evidence that bitcoins could function as real currency.

The value of bitcoin began rising again in early 2013, hitting $266 in April. The price started to drop again in May, reaching a low of $70 in June. The price hit $150 in October, $200 in November, then suddenly soared to a high of $1,242 on November 29. Again, such a rapid rise in value was at least partially attributable to irrational enthusiasm, and the price crashed down to the $500-600 range on the next month. That's a big drop from $1242, but if you had been holding on to bitcoins that were worth only $70 a few months before, you would still have been in position to make a large profit.

In January 2014, the value of bitcoin went up and down within the $750-1000 range, but then the Mt. Gox disaster hit. Despite temporary ups and downs, bitcoin has clearly been rising steadily in value from the beginning, but it's not surprising that the fall of Mt. Gox caused a huge loss in confidence. Prices dropped down to $550 over the next month, and continued to fall as rumors spread about a possible ban on bitcoin in China. The overall lack of confidence in cryptocurrency lasted about a year, bringing bitcoin down to a value of $200 in March 2015. Then the price finally started to rise again, stabilizing around $600 in summer 2016. Another sudden spike to

$1,150 in January 2017 was followed by a predictable fall to $750, but then prices began to steadily climb over several months. On June 12 2017, the price of bitcoin reached $3,000, and now hovers around $12,000.

As you can see from this brief history, volatile phases seem to occur when investors get carried away and the price goes up too much, too soon. If you can sell during the bubble you'll obviously come out ahead, but don't count on any sudden jump in price to last for long. Holding out for an even higher price will probably backfire after a certain point.

Longer declines in bitcoin prices have occurred when investor confidence was badly shaken by regulatory worries or a crisis like what happened to Mt. Gox. If you hold on to your bitcoins through the downturn, they should start to rise in value again after a little while. Despite the volatility of bitcoin, the overall trend has been up and up, and even events like the Silk Road crackdown don't seem to have had a huge effect on investor interest in bitcoin.

Bitcoin Investment Risks

If you're investing in bitcoin without buying bitcoins yourself, there are some additional risks to be aware of. For instance, bitcoin investment funds are often traded "over-the-counter," a status shared with penny stocks and other risky investments. Buying over-the-counter investments is not an inherently bad idea, but you should be aware that this type of investment is less closely regulated and therefore riskier. Funds traded over-the-counter are required to provide far less information, but there are things you can look out for.

One thing to check is whether shares in your bitcoin investment fund are selling for more or less than the value of the bitcoins themselves. It's common for funds to trade for around 4.5% less than the value of their own net assets, and that shouldn't be seen as a warning sign in and of itself. Some funds trade for a premium, meaning that shares in the fund cost a bit more than the net assets of the fund are actually worth. That is also not a warning sign.

However, if a fund is trading for much more or much less than the value of its net assets, you should be highly cautious. For example, Bitcoin Investment Trust shares were selling for $531 a share in May 2017, when a BIT share represented 0.093 bitcoin. Based on the value of a bitcoin at the time, BIT shares were selling for 105% of the value of the bitcoins in the fund. This led Jordan Wathen at *The Motley Fool* to describe BIT as "the worst way to buy bitcoin" at that time. In Wathen's view, such a steep premium could only mean that the shares were overvalued. As of June 2017, the BIT premium still stood at 55%.

Uncertainty

Because bitcoin is so new, many aspects of bitcoin's future cannot be predicted with any confidence. Governments are still adjusting to the concept of bitcoin and have not really settled on a regulatory approach. To give one example of how volatile this could be, just imagine the effect on bitcoin's value if the Chinese government suddenly decided to ban cryptocurrency. Mere speculation that this could happen has already driven one downturn on the bitcoin markets.

About one out of every three bitcoin exchanges have been successfully targeted by hackers, in some cases resulting in massive losses as in the Mt. Gox situation. The possibility of losing your entire investment to a clever hacker and an exchange with lax security policies is a real concern.

Bitcoin was the first successful digital currency, but it isn't the only one. What if another cryptocurrency turns out to be more popular over the long term? This concern has led some investors to diversify, buying not only bitcoins but so-called "alt-coins" such as Ethereum.

One reason bitcoin may not turn out to be the most successful long-term option is the issue of scalability. For bitcoin to replace fiat currency in our daily lives, it has to be able to handle a very high transaction volume with low confirmation times. The limitations to the size of a block raise the question of whether this is even possible.

One long-term concern for any bitcoin investor is the possibility that a currency designed specifically to remain decentralized will become centralized anyway. As the supply of 21 million bitcoins slowly runs out and the rewards get cut in half again and again, transaction fees are likely to increase and increase. There will probably be fewer and fewer miners as this happens, increasing the risk of the dreaded "51% attack." This describes a scenario where one person or group gains control over 51% or more of the bitcoin market. Due to the pseudo-anonymity of bitcoin and the option to create limitless numbers of bitcoin wallets, a determined conspiracy to take control of bitcoin could theoretically work even now. If someone was able to get control of bitcoin through a 51% attack, the currency would lose its features of decentralization and self-regulation. Whoever controlled the most bitcoins would control the blockchain.

As much of a disaster as this would be for bitcoin enthusiasts, the high price of bitcoin makes a 51% attack seem implausible in the foreseeable future. Anyone trying to buy control of bitcoin would need to have very deep pockets indeed.

CHAPTER 9
GETTING STARTED

If you're ready to get started with bitcoin, there are three basic steps:

- Choose your wallet

- Secure your wallet

- Choose your exchange

Once you've done these three things, you'll be ready to start buying and selling bitcoins.

Hardware Wallets

Digital Bitbox: This wallet looks a lot like a small USB flash drive, and plugs into the side of your computer in the same way. Digital Bitbox is designed to be intuitive and easy to use.

KeepKey: KeepKey has an LED screen that displays the details of your bitcoin transaction, and requires verification of each transaction shown on the screen for improved security.

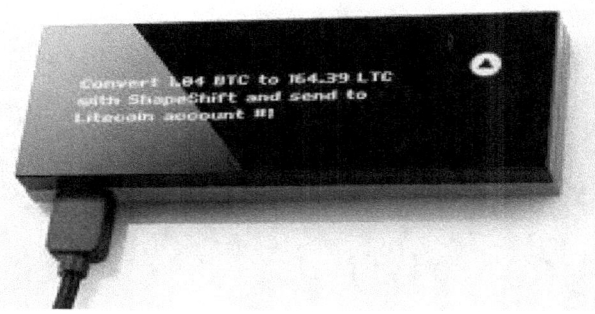

Ledger Nano: This wallet has a number of different features, including the ability to be used as a prepaid card.

Ledger Nanc S: This wallet plugs into the USB port and also has a small LED display so you can see the details of every transaction.

Trezor: Trezor is designed to keep your keys safe even if the device is plugged into a computer infected by malicious software. This gives you some of the safety of cold storage, but still allows you to sign transactions while connected to the internet.

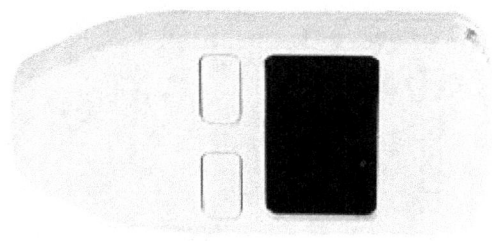

Software Wallets

ArcBit: This is one of the more intuitive wallets, so it might be a good choice for someone new to bitcoins.

Armory: This is more of an expert's wallet, with encryption and backup options not found in most.

Bitcoin Core: Bitcoin Core is a particularly secure, stable and private platform for your bitcoins, but does not have some of the features of other wallets.

Bitcoin Knots: Bitcoin Knots is also very secure, stable and private, and offers more features. However, it does have the disadvantage of using high levels of memory.

Bitcoin Wallet: An intuitive option for people without strong technical skills.

Bither: This wallet offers both hot and cold storage modes, allowing you to emphasize security or convenience as needed.

Breadwallet: Breadwallet is designed to be a "standalone" option, meaning that it has no server of its own that could potentially be hacked.

BTC.com: BTC is another intuitive wallet, and offers support for local languages and currencies.

Coin Space: This is a free online option, perfect for getting started and for storing small amounts for daily purchases.

Copay: This wallet allows you to have multiple wallets on the same account, and to share wallets with other users.

Electrum: This wallet is fast, easy to use and allows the use of secret pass phrases.

GreenBits: GreenBits is also designed to be easy and fast, and also allows you to set spending limits.

mSigna: This wallet is probably best suited for business use, offering features and scalability beyond what the average user would probably need. However, the software is still reasonably intuitive to use.

Xapo: Xapo is a wallet that also offers a cold storage option, and its own debit card that uses bitcoins.

Paper Wallets and Bitcoin Tokens

Gimmicky paper wallets designed to look like real wallets don't really work any differently than a simple sheet of notebook paper with your bitcoin keys on it. Bitcoin tokens (which look like coins) are also just a medium for storing the encryption keys that allow you to access your bitcoins in the blockchain. They are safer than simply storing your keys in an online wallet, but if you enter your key online to complete a transaction there is still a window of opportunity in which you could potentially be hacked.

Securing Your Wallet

We've already discussed many of the "best practices" you should follow to secure your wallet, but for ease of use here they are in the form of a list:

- Keep most of your bitcoins offline, in a hardware wallet or cold storage.

- Select a wallet that offers two-factor authentication to deter hackers. (Requiring both a password and an email for access, for example.)

- Don't keep any more money in a hot wallet than you would in a physical wallet.

- Backup your wallet in multiple locations – for instance, on paper at your home, on a USB drive at your office and on a CD in your car. Make sure to backup all your keys – it can be easy to miss some! Encrypt any backups you keep online.

- Use a strong password when you set up your wallet. Anything that can be easily guessed can be easily hacked, but hackers can also break any password using words that can be found in the dictionary. That's why people take additional steps like replacing some of the letters with numbers or symbols.

- Use offline signing only when accessing your savings. In other words, if you need to spend more than the amount you would normally keep in a hot wallet, use a system that requires you to sign transactions while you are not online.

- More than one signature should always be required to access company or organization funds.

- Install all updates without delay – they often patch security vulnerabilities.

Bitcoin Exchanges

There are many options when it comes to choosing an exchange. With more than 60 trading platforms available there is sure a lot of choice. The following list shows some of the predominant platform in alphabetical order.

Bitsquare: Bitsquare, also known as Bisq, is designed to be as decentralized as Bitcoin itself. Unlike other bitcoin exchanges, it has no servers of its own and stores neither bitcoin nor any other currencies directly. Customer bitcoins are kept in external wallets that can only be accessed with multiple signatures, and other currencies are traded directly between customers rather than through bitsquare itself.

Bitstamp: Bitstamp is a Slovenian exchange that offers the ability to exchange bitcoins and dollars instantly, as well as the ability to conduct limit orders in a range of currencies.

Bitfinex: This exchange keeps only 5 percent of its assets in hot wallets, with the remainder in cold storage for security. Bitfinex also offers options such as short selling and margin trading, such as you would expect to find when trading on the stock market. Ever since the collapse of Mt. Gox, Bitfinex has been the dominant exchange in the bitcoin ecosystem. Although Bitfinex has also suffered losses to hackers, it has very robust security features and is the obvious choice if you're not sure which exchange appeals to you most when getting started.

BitWage: This service isn't exactly a bitcoin exchange. Instead, it's a service that allows you to pay or receive wages in the form of bitcoins. If you want to dive in to the bitcoin world, getting your paycheck in bitcoin form will certainly get you off to a running start.

BTCChina: This is the primary Chinese bitcoin exchange, and therefore one of the biggest exchanges in the world even if most users outside of China use other services. The primary fiat currency on BTCChina is the Chinese yen, but dollars are also used.

BTC-e: BTC-e is an exchange that lets you choose whether to use bitcoins or fiat currencies. Although the company claims to be based in Bulgaria, the owners are anonymous and no one is really sure who they are and where they are from. Although this may raise some issues of trust, the company does a very large volume of trade.

Coinbase: Coinbase is much more than a bitcoin exchange, because it also processes payments and provides a popular wallet service. Coinbase is structured in a different way from most bitcoin exchanges, because it requires users to link their account to a traditional bank account so that

Coinbase never hold any currency belonging to customers.

Cryptsy: If you want to try out some of the other cryptocurrencies, Cryptsy may be the way to go – it allows you to trade in bitcoin, Litecoin, Dogecoin and many others, around 200 cryptocurrencies in all. Bitcoin may be far past the days where you could acquire them for pennies and watch them grow in value every day, but that doesn't mean you can't find another currency that will do just as well!

Kraken: Kraken is a good option for expert traders, with many features not available on most other exchanges. Kraken's features allow traders to customize many details of the process to get the specific results they want, but the exchange is still used by beginners as well. You can choose Kraken right from the beginning if you want to, but another option is to start with something basic and then switch to Kraken once you have some expertise.

LocalBitcoins: LocalBitcoins is a company that facilitates person to person bitcoin exchanges. Users who want to do an in-person exchange post an advert offering their terms, and any interested parties in their local area can contact them through the site and arrange the deal. The buyer hands over the payment in cash or as a check, and the seller sends bitcoins to their designated address. If you choose to trade bitcoins this way, make sure to follow some basic safety precautions. Meet the person you want to do business with in a public place such as a café, and don't walk around with large sums of cash. If you are not quite this cautious and you agree to bring a suitcase of money to a dark alley somewhere for a bitcoin trade, don't be surprised if you wind up losing the money without getting any bitcoins!

CONCLUSION

Congratulation for making it through to the end of this book, you should now have a good understanding about bitcoin and possess all of the tools you need to achieve your goals whatever they may be.

The next step is to decide if you want to invest in bitcoin, how you'd like to go about it and how deep you want to go.

Remember that bitcoin is still an experimental currency – it was only invented in 2008. When bitcoin was first created, no one other than the wildest optimists would have predicted that it would be selling for the price it is selling for today. Some of the more extreme bitcoin enthusiasts believe that the cryptocurrency is the future of money, and will eventually replace fiat currencies around the world.

On the other hand, there are reasons to be skeptical that bitcoin will be able to remain at the top. The price of bitcoin has been volatile, and it is always possible that the whole thing could turn out to be a price bubble. Some of bitcoin's more extreme skeptics have described it as a Ponzi scheme, worthless without the misguided enthusiasm of its devotees.

In all likelihood, neither the extreme skeptics nor the extreme enthusiasts have it right. Bitcoin is a speculative investment based on a brilliant but still experimental idea.

Always be sure to consult a technical expert before making any major investments, so you make your decisions with the benefit of the best advice. Nobody can predict bitcoin's future. That's one of the things that makes bitcoin a uniquely exciting investment opportunity.

Finally, if you found this book useful in anyway, a review on Amazon is always appreciated!